TO STUDY AS KINGS

Business and Life Success Principles from a Biblical Standpoint

Jacob Lee

TO STUDY AS KINGS

Business and Life Success Principles from a Biblical Standpoint

All scripture quotations are from the King James Version (KJV).

ISBN: 979-8-9890682-3-4

Book design by Esther K. Moody

Table of Contents

Foreword
Introduction

SOWING & REAPING

FAITHFUL IN THE LEAST

BELIEF

STAND IN THE GAP
& WALK IN YOUR PURPOSE

Acknowledgments
About the Author

Foreword

To Study as Kings takes a straightforward approach to studying biblical principles. It is for the Kingdom-minded person who wants to understand the truth of how to view business and finances.

The truth is, Jacob has walked the way from poverty to prosperity. With his life-changing mindsets, he has mapped the steps to a prosperous Christian business life bringing us *To Study as Kings*.

Many books have pages and pages of filler, but *To Study as Kings* has no fluff. Here you will find clear concepts for Christian Prosperity, simply stated to help open your mind to the truth about finances. Even before you reach the end of this book, you will be able to practice what you've learned in your everyday life.

The truth about God and money has been lost to many. However, once understood, the Bible is clear and speaks of prosperity as a gift and blessing of God. This book helps bring this into perspective, freeing your mind to prosper as only those blessed of the Lord can do.

May these blessings of truth, understanding, and prosperity become clear to you as you take your own journey to search out these matters, studying as kings.

—Daniel Lee

say things well. Why do you think we listen to music? Why are some speeches so extremely impactful while others just don't pack a punch? Because when we say things with our heart and emotion, people listen—even if it is not the truth.

Words are the superpower of humanity! The Bible says, "Death and life are in the power of the tongue" (Proverbs 18:21). By our words, we can kill people, spiritually or physically.

It is not my goal to get you to believe me, but my goal is for you to study it out and see if it is so, like they did in Acts 17:11 where it says: "These were more noble than those in Thessalonica, in that they received the word with all readiness of mind, and searched the scriptures daily, whether those things were so."

In order to study the Bible correctly, I believe there are several rules we need to follow to understand the real message.

Three rules of the Bible by Myron Golden, host of the *Bible Success Secrets* podcast:

1. *The law of context.* The verse cannot contradict other verses or then we are not understanding it correctly.

2. *The law of definition.* We must look up every word in the original language to really understand what the author is trying to communicate.

3. *The law of first mention.* The first mention of any principle is the original plan that God set up.

There is not my truth or your truth. There is only THE truth. God's word is truth. In fact, the original Greek word for faith means several things. First, it means "moral conviction," and second, it means, "the system of truth." The Bible is the system of truth we can rely on.

Introduction

In the beginning was the Word, and the Word was with God, and the Word was God.

—John 1:1

"And God said, Let there be light: and there was light" (Gen. 1:3). Wow, what an amazing statement!

The power of the spoken word is such an amazing power, wielded by some to good, and some to bad.

It is used by dictators to spread indoctrination. It is used by great leaders to inspire. It is used by evangelists to give hope to the hopeless. It is used in politics like tanks and machine guns on a battlefield. It is used by the comforters of the heartbroken. It is used by you and me to communicate our thoughts. And most importantly it is used by God to communicate with us.

Have you ever wondered what is special about humanity? Have you ever considered the difference between us and monkeys or other animals? It really comes down to one thing—words.

Words are spiritual. We can speak to inspire, amaze, or tear down.

Speech has a much deeper meaning than just the simple words we use. It does something to our spirit when people

I love the Bible so much and the amazing wisdom it contains, and I hope I can inspire you to read and study it more. It is like a treasure chest that is endless. And every time you open it there is a new treasure inside.

What I will share in this book are things I have learned in my own life. I believe it is all accurate, but some things are opinion and open to interpretation. In the end, you will need to form your own opinion on subjects.

The Bible says, "Without counsel purposes are disappointed: but in the multitude of counsellors they are established" (Proverbs 15:22). I believe the point is not to get a massive amount of advice as much as it is about getting multiple viewpoints. And I hope I can be one of those.

SECTION I

Sowing & Reaping

Chapter 1

The Principle of Sowing and Reaping

Turn again our captivity, O Lord, as the streams in the south. They that sow in tears shall reap in joy. He that goeth forth and weepeth, bearing precious seed, shall doubtless come again with rejoicing, bringing his sheaves with him.

—Psalm 126:4-6

Everything affects everything! Not a very scientific term, but it is true despite that.

There are no exceptions. Everything is linked together. Every action, every thought, has a consequence. It is the law of sowing and reaping.

Every thought is like a little seed. And the aggregate of those thoughts will define the actions you take, and the aggregate of those actions will determine how your life works out. The Bible says, "Be not deceived; God is not mocked: for whatsoever a man soweth, that shall he also reap" (Galatians 6:7).

It is a very simple principle, yet so easy to overlook. It does not have to be complicated. It is quite easy to act upon. Sometimes just being aware of it will help you make better decisions.

For years I would hear people saying, "You need to follow your *'why.'*" I do agree with that. But it can take a while to put that into a single thought or idea. For me, my *"why"* is simply to serve the people around me. In every word I say and every action I take, I will serve in some way.

When I am on the phone, I will give people the best advice I can possibly give them. I will encourage people with my words on my podcast, on social media, in conversations, and in small actions I take every day. It may be as simple as giving a child a glass of cold water.

Since my life is dedicated to serving others, I don't have to have grand plans, but in simple daily actions, I can strive to consistently give value to others.

That is not very difficult. It is the ideal by which I strive to live my life. I am sure you can find something equally simple for yourself. My personal business mantra comes from Luke 16:10 in the Bible: "He that is faithful in that which is least is faithful also in much; and he that is unjust in the least is unjust also in much." I will go into more detail later in the book about that verse all on its own.

There are many laws that govern the universe, laws that are so incredibly powerful. So powerful, in fact, that violating one or more of them can virtually guarantee failure, and application of them can virtually guarantee success in almost any endeavor.

One of these laws is so tightly linked with everything else that it is impossible to get away from it.

It is called the law of sowing and reaping.

There are no actions that are exempt from this law. Everything from my marriage to my finances, my very existence, and my relationship with Jesus is inextricably linked to this law.

The Bible has talked about it for thousands of years, but scientists have "rediscovered" it as the law of cause and effect. "For every action in nature, there is an equal and opposite reaction ..." Or we could say every reaping comes from sowing, and every sowing has a reaping.

I have been blessed with such an incredible marriage! And one of the reasons my marriage is good is I actively apply this principle to it. When I look for little ways to genuinely compliment my wife and at the same time avoid criticizing her, it has an incredible effect on my marriage.

There are several principles that also intertwine. The first is obviously the law of sowing and reaping. Then there's being faithful in small things, being consistent, and having exponential returns.

The first principle of sowing and reaping is a component of everything, without exception. And in order to explain it in more detail, I will use farming analogies.

There is no reaping without sowing. Even for people who reap things they did not plant, someone or something caused it to be sowed.

There is almost always a lot of work involved with sowing good seed. For example, tilling the ground, killing weeds, and removing pests and stones. All of these are important to get good ground to sow the seed.

It is the same way in business. If we want to do a marketing campaign, for example, we will need a phone number, business cards, website, social media presence, and Google listing, just to name a few. It will vary widely by industry, but marketing will be significantly less effective without proper preparation.

There are seasons involved with any crop. Spring is when the planting is done, and summer is when fertilizing is done and the crop must be protected. In fall the harvesting is done, and winter is where you rest and prepare again for the spring.

As on a farm, so also in business. A team is needed to operate it successfully. A great team can make a big difference in how your crop turns out. A bad team will not spray the weeds when they need to, or take care of the pests when they need to, or bring the crop out of the fields when the weather turns bad.

A great team can mean the difference between having enough for the winter or just getting by. It is exactly how John Maxwell would say, "Everything rises and falls on leadership."

There will be storms for any farmer. Sometimes they may damage the crop. And that is exactly like it is in business. There are often circumstances outside of our control, but just because a hailstorm comes up and beats the farmers' crops to the ground does not mean that farming does not work.

Yet in business, so many times people say something does not work simply because one or two tries fail to get it moving. That is the perfect time to analyze and see what we are doing wrong. I have seen many people quit just as things were about to succeed.

As I will mention in further chapters, a farmer maintains urgency throughout the year. First, an urgency in the spring to get the crops into the ground, then an urgency to get the fertilizer on the crop at the best time, and finally an urgency to harvest the crops in the fall before it rains or snows on them.

In our business, it is also very important to maintain a sense of urgency. An urgency to deal with problems before they get too big, an urgency to maintain growth, an urgency to be looking for ways to grow, an urgency to learn, and an urgency to become better leaders.

When we become complacent, the business will eventually decline. I will talk more about being faithful in small things in a later chapter, but this also applies to farming. All things are composed of small things. It is tightly linked with the law of sowing and reaping.

My personal business mantra comes from Luke 16:10, "He that is faithful in that which is least is faithful also in much; and he that is unjust in the least is unjust also in much." I believe there is an implied blessing in that verse that if we do the small things faithfully, we will be given greater blessings, and if we do not, we won't be given greater blessings.

The cornerstone of any success rests on small actions taken over and over. Those actions must come from our identity where we literally do what we do because of who we are. If I'm an honest person, I will always act with integrity, but if I don't have integrity, I will not act from an identity of integrity.

In summary, there are several points to sowing and reaping that I believe are essential.

1. Sowing and reaping are cause and effect.

2. There are seasons.

3. There will be storms.

4. We need to maintain a sense of urgency.

"They that sow in tears shall reap in joy. He that goeth forth and weepeth, bearing precious seed, shall doubtless come again with rejoicing, bringing his sheaves with him" (Psalm 126:5-6).

"The wicked worketh a deceitful work: but to him that soweth righteousness shall be a sure reward. As righteousness tendeth to life: so he that pursueth evil pursueth it to his own death" (Proverbs 11:18-19).

"Verily, verily, I say unto you, Except a corn of wheat fall into the ground and die, it abideth alone: but if it dies, it bringeth forth much fruit" (John 12:24).

Chapter 2

Sowing & Reaping: Spring

Don't judge each day by the harvest you reap but by the seeds you plant.

—Robert Louis Stevenson

When it comes to sowing and reaping, one of the most important facets is simply to understand the seasons.

Spring is a time for preparing the ground, planting, and focusing.

Every business has a cycle, and every business has a spring cycle. It is not always the cycle where production is the highest but it's where the preparation is done for the crop.

On a farm, the first thing in spring is to prepare the soil. In our business, this might look like branding, building or updating our website, updating social media, networking, and following up with existing relationships. It doesn't always directly bring in new clients, but it does make them aware of you or make it possible to find you if they are looking for your product or service.

The second thing you do in spring on a farm is to plant the seeds. This is something that will vary based on the business. In my business, it will look like social media marketing, networking, direct mail marketing, cold calling, and trade shows.

In my business, the planting season is long. Most of the year, in fact. But by far the best time is early in the year. People are planning on how much money they will be spending on their projects for the year and allocating money to those projects.

The mindset of the farmer in the spring is focused. In our businesses, we need to be focused and aware of the best time to be "planting." The farmer does not go on a two-week vacation right in the middle of planting. And neither should we.

We need to have urgency in the spring just like the farmer. He must prepare the ground before it is warm or dry enough or wet enough to plant, depending on climate and crop.

He has a sense of urgency about getting his ground prepared before he starts planting. He has a sense of urgency about getting the seeds in the ground when the weather is warm enough. If he doesn't get the crop out soon enough, the weeds will take over the field. If he doesn't get the seeds out soon enough, he won't have enough time to harvest in the fall before it is too cold or the prices drop too low.

We need that kind of urgency in our business. An urgency to get to the customer before he calls your competition. An urgency to deal with problems our customers are facing so they can be reliant on our products or services. An urgency to take advantage of opportunity when it comes around. An urgency to grow and become better at serving our clients.

In our business, we instituted a very simple policy. When we get a call from a customer who needs an estimate on their roof, our goal is to be on the roof within 48 hours. Once we finish the inspection, our goal is to have an estimate in their hands within another 48 hours at the latest. We did not ironclad the policy, but that was the goal.

Of course, if a customer requests a different time, then we would always accommodate them to the best of our ability. But we noticed a correlation between how fast they had an estimate in their hand and the percentage of projects we would win. There is a book written by Jason Jennings in 2002 called *It's Not the BIG That Eat the SMALL ... It's the FAST That Eat the SLOW*. I'll be honest; I haven't read the book yet, but the title caught my eye and got me thinking about that statement. That is the urgency we need to have. Urgency is a major competitive advantage for any company.

Spring to some companies will look very different from a farm. If you make Christmas ornaments, they will look very different compared to the person who digs gold in Alaska or does roofing in Maine.

Understanding the seasons for your company or organization is imperative for understanding your market.

So, if you take the time to think about your business and what "spring" looks like to you, it may help you serve your customers more effectively and help you to understand your market better.

To summarize spring:

1. Planting seeds is like advertising.

2. Focus and urgency are essential in the spring.

3. We need to prepare the ground.

Chapter 3

Sowing & Reaping: Summer

He that gathereth in summer is a wise son: but he that sleepeth in harvest is a son that causeth shame.

—Proverbs 10:5

A farmer in the summer has several jobs. Protecting his crop from animals, protecting his crop from weeds, and making sure his crop has enough nutrients to grow. Just to name a few.

There are several parallels in business. Any undertaking in business has things that are needed to keep it operating smoothly. Great customer service is like fertilizer. Even though it does not directly get a new customer in the door, it will certainly make the average customer spend significantly more on your products and services and be much more loyal to your business.

The Gold standard of customer service comes from the Bible, when Jesus said, "And as ye would that men should do to you, do ye also to them likewise" (Luke 6:31).

After all, isn't serving the customer all about looking at it from their point of view and doing your absolute best to make them happy?

When it comes to protecting the crop, the farmer has many different tools depending on the crop, the pests, and the weeds. In the same way, you need to understand the "weeds" and "pests" that want to destroy or eat your crop and the tools needed to protect it.

There is a parable that Jesus talked about in the Bible that might shed some light on this:

"And he spake many things unto them in parables, saying, Behold, a sower went forth to sow; And when he sowed, some seeds fell by the wayside, and the fowls came and devoured them up: Some fell upon stony places, where they had not much earth: and forthwith they sprung up, because they had no deepness of earth: And when the sun was up, they were scorched; and because they had no root, they withered away. And some fell among thorns; and the thorns sprung up, and choked them: But other fell into good ground, and brought forth fruit, some an hundredfold, some sixtyfold, some thirtyfold. Who hath ears to hear, let him hear" (Matthew 13:3-9).

Now our first instinct is to drive away all the animals from the field. For simple things like bugs, we spray pesticides or other deterrents on the crop to keep them off.

If you notice in the parable, it does not say the farmer ran after the birds. The birds are kind of like our competition. They fly in and try to take any seeds we have been planting. Trying to undermine our advertising efforts or our credibility. But there is little point in going after them because guess what? When we go after them, we leave the field.

There is nothing wrong with building a fence around the field to keep out the critters. But at some point, it is better just to plant so much that it will not majorly affect our crop.

The thorns will occasionally start growing in our fields and it will choke the life of some of the plants. We cannot get so bogged down with these problems that we forget to continue sowing more seed. We can plant ten times as much in the time it would take to deal with the thorns.

In our businesses, this is such an important part to think about. We can complain about taxes, licensing and permits, workers comp, and a hundred other things, or we can buckle down and deal with it.

It is just a distraction to try to change the way it is. The majority of problems in a business will go away if there are just more sales. Why not overwhelm the thorns with growth? Grow a crop so massive a few thorns do not even matter.

Now finally, the rose in the cornfield. Imagine a beautiful rose in the middle of a cornfield. It is big and healthy and vibrant and the most beautiful rose you ever saw. What is that rose to the farmer? Well, it is a weed. It is stealing nutrients from the corn and will be eliminated just like all the other weeds.

There are many things in a business that are like that rose. People do many good things that are like that rose. For myself, a good example would be if I joined the fire department. Would it be a good thing? Absolutely. Would it harm my business? Absolutely. For me, that is a rose in my cornfield.

I cannot operate my company and still be there for the community in the capacity of a fireman. Or it might be investing in things that do not help my main business before it is running on its own.

If I want to grow roses, then I need to have the right equipment, the right knowledge, and the right markets before I plant a whole field of roses. But not when I'm a corn farmer.

A lot of people invested in cryptocurrencies. And a lot of people lost money. A lot made some money but very few made a lot of money. For myself, this is a rose in the cornfield. I don't have the time or knowledge that it would take to properly make money with it. So, I avoid it.

That is a lens that is important in business. Will it help my current business? Is the ROI as good as my business and can my business run without me? It is impossible to run after two rabbits at the same time.

It is exactly like the Bible says, "No man can serve two masters: for either he will hate the one, and love the other; or else he will hold to the one, and despise the other. Ye cannot serve God and mammon" (Matthew 6:24).

Being focused is essential to grow a great crop or have a successful business.

People often talk about work-life balance. The problem with balance is averaging out your time between multiple things. You cannot be focused and balanced at the same time.

As Myron Golden would say, "Focus is a season and balance is a season." Each has their time. Summer is a season for focus.

To summarize summer:

    1. Fertilizing the crop is important. It is like great customer service.

2. Killing weeds is important to keep them from choking the crop. Weeds are like distractions. Like a rose in the cornfield.

3. Protect our crops from wildlife. Develop relationships with our clients so competition doesn't have a chance to take them.

Chapter 4

SOWING & REAPING: FALL

And let us not be weary in well doing: for in due season we shall reap, if we faint not.

—Galatians 6:9

The fall is a time of harvest for a farmer. He is not on vacation or giving in to other distractions because the wildlife will eat his crop. Or it might start raining and snowing before his crop is in. He is focused on bringing his crop in.

In business, when things are going well, when sales are coming in hot and fast, and you can barely cash checks quickly enough, it is not the time to go on vacation. The momentum is essential to maintain. If you must take a break, keep it as short as possible.

Why is that? Why should we have this sense of urgency? It is simple. Winter is coming! And we must prepare.

After a strong economy comes what? That's right, a weak one. But after a weak one comes what? A strong one! We must be prepared when everything is going well because winter is coming.

One of my all-time favorite verses on this subject comes from the Bible in Proverbs 6:6-8, "Go to the ant, thou sluggard; consider her ways, and be wise: Which having no guide, overseer, or ruler, Provideth her meat in the summer, and gathereth her food in the harvest."

First off it says, "Having no guide, overseer, or ruler," which means being self-disciplined. We must do what we need to do without waiting for somebody to tell us we must. To develop the capacity within ourselves to do the things that we know we must without external motivation. Without self-discipline, we do not have the capacity to be truly successful.

Second, the ant is laying up for the winter. We must prepare for the future when the harvest is good, and lay up for the tough times that are coming. The ant thinks to itself, "Winter is coming, and if I do not provide for that time, I will starve."

We need to have that kind of mindset in our life and business where we think about events that could happen in the future that could put us out of business. Also consider what has happened in the past in similar companies, and what we can do to prepare our company to be able to survive that.

Farmers must pay their yearly expenses out of this year's crop. So, they must store up for the future. And that is exactly how we need to be in our companies.

Thirdly, the ant thinks of more than just itself and is part of a team. It thinks about the future of its community and family. The preparation is not purely selfish, but it is also for the "team."

In an entrepreneurial setting we need to help those around us and seek to hang out with those who will do the same.

One thing the farmer has to do is put his crop in a safe place so scavengers and thieves can't get to it. We need to do the same with the savings we put aside for our companies. We need to find a way to protect it and keep it from being used elsewhere and endangering the company.

It is essential for all people but especially for business owners to be thinking of the future in all their dealings. It is important to be willing to take a short-term loss for a long-term gain or invest in something now that will pay off exponentially in years to come.

We always reap later and greater than what we sow. Every action will multiply results over time whether it is negative or positive. One corn seed can produce a full ear of corn, and one bad action can ruin your credibility for years.

Chapter 5

Sowing & Reaping: Winter

While the earth remaineth, seedtime and harvest, and cold and heat, and summer and winter, and day and night shall not cease.

—Genesis 8:22

Winter for farmers is quite relaxing if they have put away enough to survive. It is a time to rejuvenate and plan the upcoming year. The Bible says, "Thou shalt not muzzle the ox when he treadeth out the corn" (Deuteronomy 25:4). Maybe just enjoy the harvest.

Rest is sometimes doing something that is a break in routine. For example, the disciples in John 21:3 said, "Simon Peter saith unto them, I go a fishing. They say unto him, We also go with thee. They went forth and entered into a ship immediately, and that night they caught nothing."

Or the many times Jesus would go out into the desert and pray. I certainly need to get away and pray once in a while, even in the summer.

It is a time to consider the fields and the harvest and plan the next one. What should we plant? Where on the farm would it grow best? Then do the research on methods. It is a time of learning.

In business, this might be the slow season. In my business, I work with roofing contractors to build large commercial operations mostly in summer, so, for me, winter is certainly much less chaotic.

It is a time to spend with family and to prepare equipment for spring. It is a time for networking and attending conferences and trainings.

Depending on the business, attending some trade shows and developing new relationships might be in order.

Every business has a season that is like winter. It might be a month, or it might be a day of the week that is slower than others.

It is essential to understand the patterns in your business. Understanding not only your business or organization but also your industry as a whole can make a big difference in how successful your organization or company might be.

Winter is a time to set goals for the future or to develop a plan of action. As Jim Rohn would say, "Take time to gather up the past so that you will be able to draw from your experience and invest them in the future."

Winter is a time to grow personally. For myself, I do much more reading in the winter than I do in the summer.

The Bible says, "To every thing there is a season, and a time to every purpose under the heaven" (Ecclesiastes 3:1).

When it comes to personal development, I believe there are several ideas that can help us be more effective. I will share the rules I use for myself, but I'm sure there are many more. The main thing is to figure out what works for you.

My Six Rules for Personal Development:

1. Use the 80/20 rule.

2. Psalm 1:1 applies. ("Blessed is the man who walketh not in the counsel of the ungodly...")

3. Look at everything from different points of view.

4. Don't waste time reading what doesn't apply.

5. Focus on quality over quantity.

6. Without action, personal development is wasted.

The 80/20 rule is simple. It was originally called the Pareto Principle, named after Vilfredo Pareto, who was an Italian sociologist and economist. He observed that 80% of the land was owned by 20% of the people. And it was further studied by many universities and used by companies like Microsoft, who found that by fixing the top 20% of the most reported bugs, 80% of the problems would go away.

There are thousands of examples from companies and nonprofits and government organizations that have seen similar results.

This simplifies my personal development. I focus 80% of personal development on the top 20% of problems in my own life which will make 80% of the difference. I read books and articles and listen to podcasts and attend conferences that improve the most important 20% in my business and life. And the other 20% of personal development on the rest.

Second, Psalm 1:1 applies. Psalm 1:1 says, "Blessed is the man that walketh not in the counsel of the ungodly, nor standeth in the way of sinners, nor sitteth in the seat of the scornful."

If advice or a book is "ungodly," then I can throw it out. Any book or author that teaches things against biblical principles I can throw out. It is a simple but effective way to weed out many books. And besides, as Christians, do we really want to be reading things that go against everything we believe?

Third, look at everything from different points of view. The Bible says in Proverbs 15:22, "Without counsel purposes are disappointed: but in the multitude of counsellors they are established."

I don't believe it is saying the majority is right, but instead it is saying there is safety from considering many points of view. Therefore, I read from several authors on any given subject to get a broader view of it. And I believe that is what Solomon was referring to in this verse.

Even the Bible was written from different points of view, which makes it much richer and more fun to read.

Fourth, don't waste time reading the whole book if all the information is in the first three chapters. Most books on the market today front-load their books. As much as 90 percent of the information is in the first three chapters.

Discerning when to stop reading and then skimming the rest of the book can save a considerable amount of time. Not that the rest of the information won't be relevant in the future, but that is why you need a library. You can put it back on the shelf and read the rest when it becomes more applicable to you.

Fifth, focus on quality over quantity. This helps with deciding which books are the best to read. Five minutes with Elon Musk or five hours with your broke cousin. Which is better for your financial future?

There is nothing wrong with skimming through many books before you find one that is applicable to your current situation or the problem you may be facing in your organization.

Sixth, no amount of personal development will do it for you. The Bible says in James 2:26, "For as the body without the spirit is dead, so faith without works is dead also."

In the end, if you and I don't take action, nothing will happen.

SECTION II

Faithful in the Least

Chapter 6

The Principle of Faithful in the Least

He that is faithful in that which is least is faithful also in much: and he that is unjust in the least is unjust also in much.

—Luke 16:10

All things are made up of smaller things. Our life, our successes, our failures, our health, and even our happiness. There is nothing exempt from this fact.

Every physical thing in the universe is made up of some type of substance, whether it is stone, wood, glass, plastic, or even air. Then all that stuff is made up of atoms, which are made up of protons and neutrons, which are made up of quarks.

So far quarks are the smallest known thing in the universe to scientists. But, I believe there are things in life that cannot be measured that are much more important and have a much greater bearing on how our life works out. Things like our thoughts or ideas and inspirations. Nobody has been able to measure those. So far scientists have only been able to measure physical mass but have not been able to measure nonphysical mass.

Nonphysical mass is like electricity. Hard to quantify exactly what it is. But we know what it does and how to control it. It doesn't really matter what it is since we can control it and we can see what it does.

That is exactly how our thoughts and intentions work. We can't always quantify everything exactly, but we know how to use it, and we know how to control it. In fact, using it correctly will make all the difference in how our lives work out.

The Bible says in Luke 16:10, "He that is faithful in that which is least is faithful also in much: and he that is unjust in the least is unjust also in much."

This Bible verse has completely changed my life and how I do everything. It is like a compass showing the way to live, and when I get off track, it shows me the way back on track.

So, in this verse it says if we are faithful in the small things, we will also be in big things. So how can we be faithful in small things? The root word coming from the original Greek means being trustworthy, or worthy of confidence.

I believe this can mean a lot of small things such as being on time for appointments, answering my phone even if I know the person is calling with a problem, and taking responsibility for issues when they come up. I answer my phone when I say I will.

I answer my phone even though I know that a customer is calling me about a problem. I take care of my problems. I show up when I say I will. I call when I say I will, and I do what I say I will do. I am always faithful to my customers for the trust they place in me and I look out for their best interests.

For example, in 2017, we got a small roof job from a new client. We did the project, and they were quite pleased with our work. A few weeks later, we got another project from the same client. We went out and did that one as soon as we could because the roof had been leaking, and they needed it done as quickly as possible. However, during the first rainstorm after we had completed the project, it leaked. In our company, we have a policy of fixing or showing up to fix a leak within 24 to 48 hours. Most of the time, we can show up the same day.

We immediately went out to look for the leak and sealed up some stuff where we thought it could be coming in. Unfortunately, that was just the beginning of our problem. Every time it rained, it leaked again, and we just couldn't figure it out. We replaced flashing and redid parts of the roof and went over the entire roof with a fine-tooth comb to see what we had missed.

It took us eight different times to figure out what was going on. The water had been coming down behind the siding and going under our roof system. Of course, with more experience, I would have noticed the problem right away before we even started the project.

During this time, we were driving home one day from another repair. I remember discussing the problem with my brother. We were tempted to give up.

I can still remember saying if we are faithful in the least, we will be faithful in much as it says in the Bible, and if we take care of these people, maybe if they get a large project, they would be willing for us to do that also. Of course, we were both a little skeptical and my brother says to me, "They'll never get a large roof." But we were both fully committed to the customer.

Once we finally fixed the roof, the company kept giving us more work. Lots of small projects. By the end of that year, they had given us 17 different projects!

After the whole mess of the leaks on that one project, I asked the head facility manager of the company why they continued to give us more work? He told me they kept on giving us work because we showed up when they called and took responsibility when there was a problem.

That fall, they gave us a call to bid on another project. That project ended up being over $1.4 million and we ended up winning it. The head facility manager told me that we won the project because we took care of our problems, not because we were the cheapest.

Honestly, problems are literally our greatest opportunity in business. We have an opportunity to show how awesome our customer service is. The best customers we have ever had are often the ones with whom we have the best chance of demonstrating our customer service. This means they had problems, and we had an opportunity to show how well we could take care of them.

Often the greatest opportunities are disguised as problems. Taking care of our clients when they have problems is, after all, what they pay us to do.

Being faithful is one of the most important things we can do in our business because it affects every part of our life.

Chapter 7

Faithful in the Least: Micro Habits

People do not decide their futures, they decide their habits and their habits decide their futures.

—F. Matthias Alexander

I believe that if we want to change effectively for the long term, it really starts with our habits. Every tiny habit builds on the next habit, and that creates an exponential multiplier of results.

For example, someone who has great eating habits but poor exercise habits will see a much greater change by starting to exercise than the guy who has bad eating habits. It is almost impossible to out-exercise a very bad diet. And vice versa, it is incredibly difficult to eat so little that you lose weight if you get no exercise.

The reality is we must build habits one by one. As each habit gets developed and sustained, it will start to have an effect not only on the new habit but also on many of your other habits as well.

It will also increase your ability to form more good habits and increase your self-confidence, self-discipline, and self-image.

It truly is exactly as Jim Rohn used to say: "Everything affects everything."

Our habits are part of the web of our life, and as more get added, the stronger it gets. But every time one gets taken or weakened, it affects all the rest. The recipe for life change is truly in the micro habits we develop.

A good example is brushing your teeth, flossing, dressing well, and making your hair look great in the morning.

One thing I have noticed from personal experience is if I look neat and dress well at the beginning of the day, it will affect my attitude toward the entire day.

For example, consider the following habits and how your day would go without them:

1. Brushing/flossing teeth

2. Neat appropriate clothes

3. Showering

4. Shaving

5. Styling your hair

6. Breakfast

7. Reading the Bible

8. Praying

9. Coffee

10. Exercise

You may argue that some of these are necessities. And that may be true, but that also does not change the fact that they are still habits.

Some of them you may do in the evening, like exercise or devotions, but consider going without in the evening if that is the case, and imagine the impact.

Our life revolves around our habits, both good and bad.

For example, avoiding 200 calories per day versus eating an extra 200 calories per day equals a 146,000-calorie difference in one year.

Saving $20 a day versus wasting $20 per day is a $14,600 difference in one year.

Imagine continuing those two habits for ten years, good versus bad.

146,000 calories is 58 days of food for an average working man's diet of 2,500 calories per day. And $14,600 is 27% of the average salary in the United States in 2022 which was $54,132.

The small habits we have are not as small as we think. They are literally the foundation of our life.

So, in conclusion, we need to carefully consider habits and be intentional about which ones we have.

Chapter 8

Faithful in The Least: Domino/Ripple Effects

While it may seem small, the ripple effects of small things are extraordinary.

—Matt Bevin

Something I recently discovered really piqued my interest. I was reading a book written by Mark Batterson called *Do It for a Day: How to Make or Break Any Habit in 30 Days.*

In this book, he was talking about the domino effect. If you take a two-inch domino, it can topple over a three-inch domino, and a three-inch domino can topple over a four-and-a-half-inch domino and so on. Continuing the trend, the twenty-eighth domino can topple the Burj Khalifa, which by the way is 2,717 feet tall, and is currently the tallest building in the world.

My thought was: What habits do I have that can topple other habits and so on till my life becomes a wreck? Or vice versa, what two-inch habit can help me develop a three-inch habit until I can develop any habit, no matter how difficult.

Big important habits can look very difficult, but by starting small, those habits can develop over time, since every habit will affect the next habit.

A good example is food. I have been losing weight recently and so far have managed to lose 20 pounds. But I was in my office one day while my wife had an appointment out of town.

Halfway through the afternoon, I ran to the kitchen to grab some water and I saw some cake sitting on the counter. So I grabbed a piece, poured milk over it, and ate it. It was delicious. (Yes, my wife is an incredibly talented cook!) Before I knew it, I ate a second piece.

I avoid sugar as much as it's reasonably possible, but I noticed something in this instance. Because I ate one piece, the second piece was easier to eat. When we break a habit a little, it makes it easier to break it more, until we completely let it go.

We need to be extremely on guard against those little ripple effects that happen with our habits. A ripple is something that happens when you drop something in liquid. The ripple affects the liquid from the point where something was dropped in.

My exercise habit takes a great deal of intentionality to not be disrupted when I travel. So, I made certain rules for myself to help. I will exercise by running two miles per day. When I am out of town, I will exercise in the hotel gym. The only time I don't exercise is when there is no gym available or I'm traveling all night. And I do not beat myself up about that.

I will never compromise my habit as long as my health allows and there are facilities available. When you travel a lot on business, you must make sure that your health habits will work with your schedule.

One thing I have noticed is the more I exercise and lose weight, the more disciplined I become with eating. It is a ripple effect of having good habits. Every habit affects the next habit and so on until it affects your entire life.

The Bible speaks of this in Ephesians 4:16, "From whom the whole body fitly joined together and compacted by that which every joint supplieth, according to the effectual working in the measure of every part, maketh increase of the body unto the edifying of itself in love."

I know for certain that if I hit my finger with a hammer, my whole body is affected. When my tooth hurts, it can hurt so badly it puts my whole body in bed. Nobody writes off a bad toothache. But we do it all the time with bad habits, and we completely sabotage our success in life by the lies we believe about ourselves.

Every bad habit is like a toothache. If we ignore it, it takes constant time and energy away from other parts of our life.

Time is our most valuable resource, so let's not waste it.

We will have a very difficult time weeding out every bad habit, but if we constantly build new ones that are good, we can develop momentum in the right direction versus the wrong one.

It's like a loaded train; in the beginning, it will take tremendous effort to notice much forward progress, but eventually, it will become virtually unstoppable. And over time, the difference in how our life works out because of those habits will exponentially multiply.

Chapter 9

Faithful in the Least: Compound Interest

The magic is doing the simple things repeatedly and long enough to ignite the miracle of the compound effect.

—Darren Hardy

So, what do I find so interesting about compound interest?

Well, it is quite simple. It was designed and instituted by God. You may ask, "How is that possible?" I'll do my best to share it with you.

In the very beginning, God created the heavens and the earth as stated in Genesis 1:1. On the third day he made trees, herbs, and grass. And how did he describe it? "Yielding fruit after his kind whose seed is in itself" (Gen. 1:11). Wow, isn't that incredible? He created plants and herbs and trees for exponential growth. It was designed by God a millennium ago, and all trees, grass, and herbs out there are still a testament to his success.

I believe that is the power of compound interest. The seed is in itself. Sow a parent seed and it grows up and creates more of itself exponentially. Now, isn't that an amazing formula? The design that God used to create the universe and everything in it, including you and I. Isn't that a clear indication he wants us to be successful?

Figuring out how to use this principle to become wealthy is the most incredible way of doing business. Warren Buffett has used this principle even though he is not a Christian. I believe we also need to seek to grow exponentially in all areas of our business. Even if it is only a 10% growth annually, exponentially it will still end up a very large sum. But imagine what would happen if you could get 50% or 100% or even higher growth.

If you can figure out how to get 20% more customers, do a 20% better job, do 20% bigger projects for 20% less waste, and continue that in your organization or company for ten years, imagine what would happen. If you only grow by 10% per year, you will double in a little less than eight years. And if you grow by 20% per year, you double in a little less than four years. If you continue for ten years at 20% growth, you grow by 600%.

In the Bible, there is a parable in Luke 19:12-26 that actually talks about multiplying what we have been given:

> 12 He said therefore, A certain nobleman went into a far country to receive for himself a kingdom, and to return.
> 13 And he called his ten servants, and delivered them ten pounds, and said unto them, Occupy till I come.
> 14 But his citizens hated him, and sent a message after him, saying, We will not have this man to reign over us.
> 15 And it came to pass, that when he was returned, having received the kingdom, then he commanded these servants to be called unto him, to whom he

had given the money, that he might know how much every man had gained by trading.

16 Then came the first, saying, Lord, thy pound hath gained ten pounds.

17 And he said unto him, Well, thou good servant: because thou hast been faithful in a very little, have thou authority over ten cities.

18 And the second came, saying, Lord, thy pound hath gained five pounds.

19 And he said likewise to him, Be thou also over five cities.

20 And another came, saying, Lord, behold, here is thy pound, which I have kept laid up in a napkin:

21 For I feared thee, because thou art an austere man: thou takest up that thou layedst not down, and reapest that thou didst not sow.

22 And he saith unto him, Out of thine own mouth will I judge thee, thou wicked servant. Thou knewest that I was an austere man, taking up that I laid not down, and reaping that I did not sow:

23 Wherefore then gavest not thou my money into the bank, that at my coming I might have required mine own with usury?

24 And he said unto them that stood by, Take from him the pound, and give it to him that hath ten pounds.

25 (And they said unto him, Lord, he hath ten pounds.)

26 For I say unto you, That unto every one which hath shall be given; and from him that hath not, even that he hath shall be taken away from him.

The first thing we see in this parable is everyone starts out equally. We have all been given something.

No two people in the world are alike. Yet God has an assignment for every person. He has given all of us gifts and abilities and a responsibility to use them. Some he has given more resources than others. And every person is responsible for what they have been given.

In Luke 12:48 it says, "... For unto whomsoever much is given, of him shall be much required: and to whom men have committed much, of him they will ask the more." The difference in how it ends out can often be attributed to small habits and decisions that exponentially multiply the results.

The second thing we see is that if we can be faithful and grow with the stuff we have, we will eventually be given much more. I believe this is talking about not just money, but also relationships, influence, and responsibilities. In the end, only those who are proven faithful get the good stuff.

The third thing we see is that the people who don't even try will lose what little bit they have. So many times, we covet what isn't ours. That is where the root of all evil comes from. 1 Timothy 6:10 talks about the love of money. What Paul was warning us about was not money, it was covetousness which is "the love of money."

It is easy to look around at other people and see what God has given them, and when we do that, guess what? We stop working with what we have already been given. Let's not bury our talent in the sand because we have only one. We can get more, but not until we first use the one we have.

I believe these things apply to our entire life. The purpose is to grow and multiply the talents, gifts, influence, and resources we have. And eventually, it will create an exponential multiplier in our life, and that is when we truly can make an impact.

SECTION III

The Principle of Belief

Chapter 10

The Principle of Belief

But let him ask in faith, nothing wavering. For he that wavereth is like a wave of the sea driven with the wind and tossed.

—James 1:6

Our belief shapes everything about us. Our actions, our identity, and how we see the world. It would be impossible to separate our beliefs from how they impact our lives. In biblical terms, faith is often used to explain belief. But the English word belief does not entirely capture what it is talking about.

Strong's Concordance (through the PocketSword app) tells us that faith comes from the Greek word πείθω {peíthō} \pi'-tho\ meaning persuasion, i.e. credence; moral conviction (of religious truth, or the truthfulness of God or a religious teacher), especially reliance upon Christ for salvation; abstractly, constancy in such profession; by extension, the system of religious (Gospel) truth itself: assurance, belief, believe, faith, fidelity.

In Hebrews 11:1 it says, "Now faith is the substance of things hoped for, the evidence of things not seen." In the original Greek, substance in this case means your support. It is literally what supports your hopes, and it is your evidence that things will come to pass. In other words, your belief and moral conviction are the evidence that it will come to pass. Your faith is the foundation of your future!

You cannot escape from this reality. You will eventually bring fruit into your life from the things you now believe. If your faith is strong, anything is possible. I love what Jesus said in Matthew 17:20. "And Jesus said unto them, Because of your unbelief: for verily I say unto you, If ye have faith as a grain of mustard seed, ye shall say unto this mountain, Remove hence to yonder place; and it shall remove; and nothing shall be impossible unto you."

In your life, you cannot escape from the consequences of your beliefs because they shape your reality and your perception of reality. You cannot act incongruent with your personal beliefs over the long term. They are your convictions. A conviction is something you believe so strongly you base your existence upon it. Thousands of Christians have been martyred for their convictions. They staked their very existence on their moral convictions.

In business, this is extremely applicable. You must make sure the beliefs you have about business are accurate or you will operate under a flawed premise. Understanding your industry in general is great. But understanding your beliefs about the business is much more important. And because business revolves around people, there is no business that exists that is exempted from this fact.

You will always act in the same way that you think, and you can only act long-term in a way that you believe. No exceptions. Even if you are an employee doing something you believe doesn't work, you will still do it because you believe that not doing it is worse than losing your job.

The Bible says in Hebrews 11:6, "But without faith it is impossible to please him: for he that cometh to God must believe that he is, and that he is a rewarder of them that diligently seek him."

So, act with boldness to accomplish your God-given purpose. Act in faith, nothing wavering. Don't doubt, instead act. God is not pleased with doubters. He wants you and I to act on the vision he has given us. We need to believe the impossible because God delights in doing amazing things that are beyond us. Believe in others, believe in the possibilities, but most of all, believe in the power of God within you.

Chapter 11

Belief: Identity

He came unto his own, and his own received him not. But as many as received him, to them gave he power to become the sons of God, even to them that believe on his name.

—James 1:6

Our identity is such an important subject. Many people have written about it in books and spoken of it on podcasts and interviews. Our identity shapes our entire life. It truly is exactly the way Ed Mylett says in his book #MaxOut Your Life (which I highly recommend): Our identity is a thermostat on our life. It keeps regulating everything we have in life from relationships to our finances.

So exactly what is this identity I'm talking about? The Merriam-Webster dictionary defines identity as, "the distinguishing character or personality of an individual."[1]

I want to start by examining scripture. Exodus 3:14 says, "And God said unto Moses, I AM THAT I AM: and he said, Thus shalt thou say unto the children of Israel, I AM hath sent me unto you."

---

[1] Merriam-Webster.com Dictionary, s.v. "identity," accessed April 8, 2023, https://www.merriam-webster.com/dictionary/identity.

It is easy to miss the significance of this statement. There is a very clear indication that "I am" is very important. In fact, when it was first used in Exodus 3, the meaning is, "to exist or to come into being."

So we could say it this way, "Existence that exists." In other words, all existence is in God. In John 1:3 it says, "All things were made by him; and without him was not any thing made that was made."

It is further strengthened in John 8:58 where it says, "Jesus said unto them, Verily, verily, I say unto you, Before Abraham was, I am."

All existence is in God: no exception. Our very being is in him and without him there is no existence. Whether we recognize it or not, whether we believe it or not, that is still the case.

That is why the Jewish leaders got so upset when Jesus said in John 8:58, "Before Abraham was, I am." They understood he said he was God and that made them incredibly angry.

Now why is all of that so important? Why am I talking about the identity of God? Other than the fact that we all are made in his image, it is simple. Our identity is rooted in God. We cannot reach our full potential without him.

God made us to need him inside of us. He wants us to become his sons. John 1:12 states, "But as many as received him, to them gave he power to become the sons of God, even to them that believe on his name."

We were designed to become God-like, or as they say among Christians, "Godly." For this reason, when we say, "I am …" and say something about ourselves, it is important to not say things that are inconsistent with the nature of God.

Instead of saying, "I am a sinner," say, "I am an overcomer," for scripture tells us: "Who is he that overcometh the world, but he that believeth that Jesus is the Son of God?" (1 John 5:5).

Instead of "I am a loser," say, "I am victorious," for scripture tells us: "But thanks be to God, which giveth us the victory through our Lord Jesus Christ" (1 Corinthians 15:57).

Instead of "I am fearful," say, "I am courageous," for scripture tells us: "Have not I commanded thee? Be strong and of a good courage; be not afraid, neither be thou dismayed: for the LORD thy God is with thee whithersoever thou goest" (Joshua 1:9).

Instead of "I am alone," say, "God is with me," for scripture tells us: "Fear thou not; for I am with thee: be not dismayed; for I am thy God: I will strengthen thee; yea, I will help thee; yea, I will uphold thee with the right hand of my righteousness" (Isaiah 41:10).

Instead of "I am unable," say, "With God all things are possible," for scripture tells us: "But Jesus beheld them, and said unto them, With men this is impossible; but with God all things are possible" (Matthew 19:26).

However, it is important that we only say the truth. I am not saying that we should ever be saying these things in untruth, but instead affirming that if the Holy Spirit lives within us these are our new characteristics.

We cannot be victorious if our own words are doing the work for the enemy. Our defense is God within us.

When we use "I AM" in a negative light, we are using the Lord's name in vain. The third commandment is: "Thou shalt not take the name of the LORD thy God in vain; for the LORD will not hold him guiltless that taketh his name in vain" (Exodus 20:7).

So in order for us to achieve more in life, we need to change how we see ourselves. Many times we subconsciously sabotage our success. Not just money and finances, but also relationships, friendships, jobs, and even our own personal happiness.

That last one is just so sad. I believe we all do it at some point in our life. A good example of it might be an exercise routine. It is not easy to exercise regularly for most, and for some people, it's challenging to eat correctly. But if we do it regularly, we feel much happier about ourselves. At least I know I always feel better about myself. And when I say no to sugar or junk food, I feel better about myself and feel better physically.

But we often self-sabotage with what we tell ourselves in the moment. Things like, "It's only 200 calories," or, "If I skip one day of exercise, it won't matter," or "I deserve this because." But if you change your self-talk to "I always exercise," and "I eat healthy," your actions will start to change.

Smokers who are quitting smoking need to have an identity shift in order to quit. If they are offered a cigarette, the response can make all the difference. If the response is, "No thanks, I'm trying to quit," they still identify as a smoker. Versus the person who says, "No thanks, I don't smoke." Two different answers, but with wildly different outcomes.

For myself, I started saying I do a two-mile run every day. I started to identify as a fit person, and within two months, I lost 20 pounds.

Something else I did to change my personal health habits was to say to myself, "I don't eat refined sugar." It still allows me to eat relatively healthy desserts and stuff with cane sugar or natural sweeteners. By changing my identity, my actions completely changed.

However, if we say these things to ourselves and don't do them, then we are lying to ourselves. My identity becomes that I'm a liar, and I don't keep my promises to myself. And that has a serious, degrading effect on any life. Therefore, it is important to always affirm the truth and always act upon it.

Affirmations can change our identity for the better, but only if it is the truth. We don't want to be living in a fantasy.

The best way to change your identity is to act the way you wish you would, then start affirming that fact to yourself and also in casual conversation with friends and family. It strengthens our belief in our actions.

After going on a run, you can now say "I'm a runner." After eating a salad instead of a donut, you can say, "I care about my health." After writing the first chapter of the book you have always wanted to write, you can say, "I'm a writer."

As long as you continue to do it regularly, the identity shift starts happening. And as long as you continue, the identity becomes stronger and stronger.

But it can also go the other way, and this is something that I learned from personal experience. When I was younger and made a mistake, I would beat myself up by telling myself things like "I was so stupid or dumb."

I had to change my identity by saying stuff like "I didn't get it right this time, but I learned a lesson," or "I am failing forward," or "If I keep trying, eventually I will figure it out."

Beating myself up over my failures made it more difficult to learn from them, but reframing what I had told myself made it easier to learn from my mistakes and made making mistakes significantly less painful.

If we look back on our life, look at the mistakes we made, and consider why we did what we did, we can learn so much about our identity. Mainly because identity is like a lens. It will distort things in certain ways, depending on what it is. You cannot see yourself differently from who you are, and the only way to change it is by becoming someone different.

Chapter 12

Belief: Internal Communication

For as he thinketh in his heart, so is he: Eat and drink, saith he to thee; but his heart is not with thee.

—Proverbs 23:7

How do you talk to yourself in the theater of your mind? Are you nice to yourself, do you praise yourself, or do you beat yourself up? This stuff is extremely important! You are the most influential person in your life. You spend more time with your own thoughts than you do with other people. So what do you tell yourself about yourself?

Think of someone close to you who you respect very highly and care very much about. How would you feel if they told you that you're a loser and a failure? Wouldn't that be devastating?

Since you are your own most influential person, don't you think that talking negatively to yourself will also have a very bad effect on your life? The Bible says in James 3:1-4:

1 My brethren, be not many masters, knowing that we shall receive the greater condemnation.
2 For in many things we offend all. If any man offend not in word, the same is a perfect man, and able also to bridle the whole body.

³ Behold, we put bits in the horses' mouths, that they may obey us; and we turn about their whole body.

⁴ Behold also the ships, which though they be so great, and are driven of fierce winds, yet are they turned about with a very small helm, whithersoever the governor listeth.

First, it says if we offend not in the word, we are perfect. If we look at the context of what it is saying, we can see that it is talking about thoughts also. My thought was how many times do we think evil? After all, our own tongue is the rudder of our ship (our body).

Every word we say will affect us. It is essential that we have positive self-talk for success in any endeavor.

In my own experience, I have noticed that those who do not know how to do something but have a very positive attitude invariably end up accomplishing way more than those who know how to do it and are negative.

Negativity is like cancer. It keeps you from being happy and keeps you from being successful. On top of that it makes life meaningless and accomplishes absolutely nothing except to make you bitter and cynical.

In Proverbs 12:25 it says, "Heaviness in the heart of man maketh it stoop: but a good word maketh it glad."

Being positive is healthy for the body. Scientists have discovered that stress and negativity are extremely harmful to the human body. They have also determined that a lack of stress is almost a guarantee of good health. And long periods of stress will create many health problems. Being positive takes intentionality. We must decide it and practice it over and over until it becomes second nature. Then, when negative things happen, our body is charged with endorphins and other chemicals that help us get over negative things faster.

Proverbs 17:22 says, "A merry heart doeth good like a medicine: but a broken spirit drieth the bones."

But when it comes to success in life by the thoughts we think, the Bible summarizes it very well in Psalm 1:1-3:

> ¹ Blessed is the man that walketh not in the counsel of the ungodly, nor standeth in the way of sinners, nor sitteth in the seat of the scornful.
> ² But his delight is in the law of the Lord; and in his law doth he meditate day and night.
> ³ And he shall be like a tree planted by the rivers of water, that bringeth forth his fruit in his season; his leaf also shall not wither; and whatsoever he doeth shall prosper.

We need to meditate on the law of God. Meditate in this instance means to ponder. This law is referring to all God's laws, both within and out of the Bible: the law of sowing and reaping, the law of being faithful in the least, and the law of gravity. Everything runs on laws. Universal laws that God created at the very beginning of creation.

In Proverb 25:2 it says, "It is the glory of God to conceal a thing: but the honour of kings is to search out a matter." God has concealed many of these secrets in his word and in nature. It is up to us to have the heart of a king and search out those secrets. God hid them so only those who seek will find them.

God wants us to be curious, which is clearly indicated by Matthew 7:7, "Ask, and it shall be given you; seek, and ye shall find; knock, and it shall be opened unto you." There are dozens of similar scriptures in the Bible.

Our thoughts are like seeds. Those seeds will spring up and grow into actions. It is important to consider those seeds that are falling on the field of the mind. Those seeds will sprout, grow up, and bear fruit. We need to be extremely intentional about the thoughts we allow into our minds. Those thoughts will become the basis of future actions. And those actions will become our life.

Luke 8:15 says, "But that on the good ground are they, which in an honest and good heart, having heard the word, keep it, and bring forth fruit with patience."

"For as he thinketh in his heart, so is he: Eat and drink, saith he to thee; but his heart is not with thee" (Proverbs 23:7).

"A wholesome tongue is a tree of life: but perverseness therein is a breach in the spirit" (Proverbs 15:4).

Chapter 13

Belief: External Communication

A man shall eat good by the fruit of his mouth: but the soul of the transgressors shall eat violence. He that keepeth his mouth keepeth his life: but he that openeth wide his lips shall have destruction.

—Proverbs 13:2-3

Words literally have the power of life and death. "Death and life are in the power of the tongue: and they that love it shall eat the fruit thereof" (Proverbs 18:21). What could possibly have a greater effect on your life than words?

Good communication is a prerequisite to succeeding in any area of life.

How can we show a customer how great our products are without good communication?

How can we show our children we love them without communication?

How can we show our spouse the depth of our love without communication?

How can we find a spouse without communication?

How can we do anything significant in life without communication?

When we communicate, we communicate with more than just words. There are things that we cannot express with words. Our nonverbal communication is just as important as the words we say. Proverbs 18:4 says, "The words of a man's mouth are as deep waters, and the wellspring of wisdom as a flowing brook."

When we speak with passion and emotion, the words we say have much more impact. Therefore a few words spoken in anger can be so damaging. Words are God-like! In fact, the Bible says, "In the beginning was the Word, and the Word was with God, and the Word was God" (John 1:1).

I think we should study great communication. We should study to become great communicators. It is our God-like superpower. Words are spiritual; they affect even our soul.

With great communication, we can inspire employees or coworkers. With great communication, we can get a great job. With great communication, we win the spouse of our dreams. With great communication, we keep that spouse in love with us.

With great communication, we can be great at sales. We can inspire people. Great leaders are usually great communicators. Maybe not even in being great at language, but in communicating their vision and emotion to other people.

Of course, communication works both positively and negatively. There is always the possibility of twisting it for dark purposes. A good example is media spin or communistic propaganda.

There are few things in life that will have as great of an effect on a person's life as words. When God created the earth, he did it with the spoken word.

As Christians, our goal is to become "Godly." In other words, "Godlike." When God created humans, what did he say? "Let us make man in our own image, after our likeness …" (Genesis 1:26). We were made to be as our creator. He created the earth by his voice. And we were created to be like him. Words are literally our superpower!

Words will shape the world around us and affect the world we live in and how we perceive it. We need to embrace our heritage as God has created us to be by becoming great at words.

Since God was the word, if we want to become godly, we must become God-like. The first action God took on earth was to speak words. He said, "Let there be light…" (Genesis 1:3).

Becoming fluent in communication is a very important part of becoming successful in business. What we tell our employees, our customers, the people we work with, and much more. The Bible spends a lot of time talking about communicating with other people and us.

Here are several scriptures on this subject:

> "Heaviness in the heart of man maketh it stoop: but a good word maketh it glad" (Proverbs 12:25).

> "These were more noble than those in Thessalonica, in that they received the word with all readiness of mind, and searched the scriptures daily, whether those things were so" (Acts 17:11).

> "By long forbearing is a prince persuaded, and a soft tongue breaketh the bone" (Proverbs 25:15).

> "He that keepeth his mouth keepeth his life: But he that openeth wide his lips shall have destruction" (Proverbs 13:3).

"He that hath knowledge spareth his words: and a man of understanding is of an excellent spirit. Even a fool, when he holdeth his peace, is counted wise: and he that shutteth his lips is esteemed a man of understanding" (Proverbs 17:27-28).

"A soft answer turneth away wrath: but grievous words stir up anger. The tongue of the wise useth knowledge aright: but the mouth of fools poureth out foolishness. The eyes of the LORD are in every place, beholding the evil and the good. A wholesome tongue is a tree of life: but perverseness therein is a breach in the spirit" (Proverbs 15:1-4).

"The lips of the wise disperse knowledge: but the heart of the foolish doeth not so" (Proverbs 15:7).

"A man hath joy by the answer of his mouth: and a word spoken in due season, how good is it!" (Proverbs 15:23).

"The thoughts of the wicked are an abomination to the LORD: but the words of the pure are pleasant words" (Proverbs 15:26).

"A man hath joy by the answer of his mouth: and a word spoken in due season, how good is it!" (Proverbs 15:23).

"The heart of the wise teacheth his mouth, and addeth learning to his lips. Pleasant words are as an honeycomb, sweet to the soul, and health to the bones" (Proverbs 16:23-24).

"Wherefore, my beloved brethren, let every man be swift to hear, slow to speak, slow to wrath" (James 1:19).

"If any man among you seem to be religious, and bridleth not his tongue, but deceiveth his own heart, this man's religion is vain" (James 1:26).

"A man shall eat good by the fruit of his mouth: but the soul of the transgressors shall eat violence. He that keepeth his mouth keepeth his life: but he that openeth wide his lips shall have destruction" (Proverbs 13:2-3).

John Maxwell says, "The words you tell yourself will affect how you believe in yourself." If you do not believe in yourself, you cannot become successful in life.

Chapter 14

Belief: Believing in Yourself

"Jesus said unto him, If thou canst believe, all things are possible to him that believeth."

—Mark 9:23

When talking about belief, there are few things more liberating than believing in yourself. I'm not talking about arrogance or brashness, but I believe that the purpose God has for your life is possible.

Even if you do not see the whole picture, you do know that God will guide your steps, and you will act with conviction toward that goal. Psalm 37:23 says, "The steps of a good man are ordered by the LORD and he delighteth in his way." When it's in our heart to truly do what is right, God will direct our path.

Self-belief, or you could say self-confidence, is essential for everyone, but especially for anyone in business or in a leadership position. You must have confidence that you can take care of the customers' needs and fix their problems if you are an entrepreneur.

If you are a leader, you must have the confidence that you can take care of your team. You need to have confidence in yourself as a leader, but your team also needs to have confidence in you. If you do not have confidence in yourself, neither will they.

As a business owner, you must have the confidence that you can sell enough products or services to keep the business afloat. And not just keep it going, but keep it thriving.

You must have the faith to act when you feel God calling you to do things that other people say are foolish or risky. When God is on your side, no one and nothing can stop you. When your purpose is a God-ordained one, "... the gates of hell shall not prevail against it" (Matthew 16:18).

The Bible is very clear that faith is a deep moral conviction and the basis of our belief. It is the very foundation of truth. "But without faith it is impossible to please him: for he that cometh to God must believe that he is, and that he is a rewarder of them that diligently seek him" (Hebrews 11:6).

Why should our faith be so strong? Because he can accomplish nothing through us if we don't have faith. Our life is completely and totally worthless without faith. We can accomplish nothing worthwhile without it. The Bible says very clearly, "For God hath not given us the spirit of fear; but of power, and of love, and of a sound mind" (2 Timothy 1:7).

So I beg of you, if you get only one point from this book, let this be the one. Don't let your life be ruined with fear and timidity, but instead embrace faith, and use the power that God has given you to overcome and persevere to accomplish the will of God in your life and the incredible purpose he has for you.

Don't let your life be lived in vain! Instead, live with a passion that comes from knowing you are not an accident.

You were designed by the almighty God of the universe, and it is his will to make you fruitful.

One of the number one reasons you need to believe in yourself is simply because Jesus did. He saw your potential before you were born. Not only did he create you, but he died that you might live, and not just live, but live fruitfully, and with the power of God within you.

Allow God to work within you, and there is nothing you cannot accomplish. As the Bible says, "Jesus said unto him, if thou canst believe, all things are possible to him that believeth" (Mark 9:23).

God is truly glorified when we allow him to work through us. It is easy to get discouraged when there's a huge task in front of us, but the reality is quite simple. When we are committed to the will of God, it gives us such freedom to rely on it and have absolute faith in his guidance.

Let's live our faith with boldness, so that we may accomplish much in our life and leave a worthwhile legacy.

Chapter 15

Belief: Believing in Others

People tend to become who you believe
them to be.

—Holley Gerth

Believing in others can often help people do more than they could ever have thought was possible. The latent potential in each one of us is much higher than we give ourselves credit for, and often other people can see it clearer than we can ourselves.

My parents' belief in me and my siblings has always been one of the things that has made us more confident adults. As a child growing up on a farm, my father had quite a bit of cattle, as well as chickens, a milk cow, goats, and various other animals. At the time, we were part of the small Amish community in northern Pennsylvania.

I believe I was six or seven when my father first taught me how to milk a cow. I was so proud of myself for managing to squeeze out a little milk. From that moment on, my brother and I were responsible for milking the cow morning and evening.

I still remember very distinctly how it felt that my father trusted us to do it. There is an innate desire in all children to please their parents, and when a parent plants a belief in their mind that they can do something, it's just amazing what they can accomplish. I was certainly no exception. That pattern was a part of my entire childhood.

It wasn't until I was a husband and a leader in business that I realized the significance in the beliefs we hold for others. Often, if we see the potential and believe in them, only then do they begin to believe in themselves. Our belief can be the catalyst that awakens their belief in their potential.

We need to be the people who, in our homes, families, and workplaces, awaken the dream in others. When we believe in others, we can often open the possibilities in their minds. Not only when things are going well for them, but also when they go through difficult times, our belief may be the only thing that will carry them through.

A perfect example comes from the Bible in Mark 2:2-5:

> 2 And straightway many were gathered together, insomuch that there was no room to receive them, no, not so much as about the door: and he preached the word unto them.
> 3 And they come unto him, bringing one sick of the palsy, which was borne of four.
> 4 And when they could not come nigh unto him for the press, they uncovered the roof where he was: and when they had broken it up, they let down the bed wherein the sick of the palsy lay.
> 5 When Jesus saw their faith, he said unto the sick of the palsy, Son, thy sins be forgiven thee.

In my mind, this is such a beautiful story. The guy is crippled so badly that he cannot even walk, so his friends carried him. Not just carried him, but ripped the roof off and lowered him into the room. As a roofing contractor, I know from experience that tearing a roof off is hard work. It just shows the remarkable faith his friends had.

Then it says, "Jesus, seeing their faith, healed him." I want to point it out very clearly. It does not say his faith, it says "THEIR" faith. The sick man may have had no faith, but his friends sure did.

We need to be like those friends of his. And wow! What incredible friends they were. Imagine yourself in that poor guy's shoes and how he felt afterward. My prayer is that I can be like those friends, and also that the people around me believe in me like that.

Another lesson from those few verses. It is simple, we need to put people in front of Jesus so he can heal them. That is one of the reasons prayers are so powerful. When we pray for people, we are like the friends of that crippled guy, by prayer lifting them to Jesus.

We need to pray relentlessly for the people in our life. God wants us to pray unceasingly with everything in our hearts. "Pray without ceasing" (1 Thessalonians 5:17).

Mary Kay Ash from Mary Kay Cosmetics once said, "You can praise almost anyone to success." Looking for and praising the correct actions will reinforce the correct actions. But it will also do something much more powerful—it will help awaken the possibilities in their own mind. This is something anyone can do.

Chapter 16

Belief: Goals & Course Correction

And the Lord answered me, and said, Write the vision, and make it plain upon tables, that he may run that readeth it.

—Habakkuk 2:2

When it comes to goals, there are many misconceptions. First off, a goal is not necessarily going to make you do more than you would otherwise do.

Unfortunately, I say this from personal experience. Just writing it down and saying I will do this does not make me do what it takes. Before you know it, the end of the year rolls around, and it's still not accomplished.

This is not the case for all my goals, but for some of them, it seems like they just don't get done.

I've come to learn that there is more to goal setting than just writing down what you want to accomplish. But it isn't nearly as hard as we make it out to be. Most goals are great but lack a few essential components.

There are several things I have learned from my experiences so far. These are by no means an exhaustive list but instead are the ones I have the most personal experience with.

1. Goals without actions are a fantasy.

2. Don't go against the grain.

3. The 80/20 rule applies.

First, goals without actions are a fantasy. A goal by itself rarely inspires you to accomplish it unless it is small and not terribly hard to attain. In order to achieve your goal and make it more than just a fantasy, you must have a plan.

You might ask, "What plan are you talking about?" That is a very simple thing to answer. All you need is an action plan. Something you can do daily to work toward your goal until you hit it.

This reaches into sowing and reaping. Almost any worthwhile accomplishment can be backtracked to how it was done. All you must do is figure out how to repeat what it takes to achieve that.

You need to figure out how long it takes to accomplish it, what skills you need, what resources it will take, who needs to be on the team, and what you currently have toward those needs, and then develop an action plan based on time.

This is an area that I have certainly not perfected but recently realized that I was lacking. I would write down something I wanted to accomplish but would often fall short of the goal. I now know the reason they never were accomplished was quite simple. I had no actionable plan to achieve that goal. If you cannot determine an action to take to achieve something toward the goal, then it is virtually impossible to achieve except by dumb luck. And I don't want dumb luck to be my strategy.

I personally believe goals should be more about action than they should be about the end goal.

Secondly, on goals, don't go against the grain if you can avoid it. It is like a rocket taking off from earth. It has a curve that makes it easier to escape the earth's gravity.

Going straight up until you reach space is probably impossible with the earth's current technology and also would be extremely inefficient. Planes are a similar example. A plane taking off never goes straight up. The amount of energy that it would take would be incredibly inefficient. Instead, a plane leverages momentum and air pressure to gain altitude.

Instead of trying to go straight at a goal, we need to understand how to leverage our strengths and build momentum, and often only then can we get off the ground in that goal.

It is very important to figure out what works for you.

For me, when I decided I wanted to lose weight and get in shape, I would try to exercise in the morning. Unfortunately, I was going against the grain for myself. It was much easier for me to exercise in the evening.

So now I have developed a habit where I always exercise in the evening no matter how late it ends up being by the time I get home. I will still exercise with very few exceptions. This means that occasionally on my road, you will see me running at two o'clock in the morning.

The point I'm trying to make is that you need to make an action plan that you can implement into your life in a way that will create the least resistance. It is an essential part of developing a workable goal.

Thirdly, the 80/20 rule applies. I wrote a little about this in Chapter 5. Develop an action plan that uses your best strengths and makes the greatest difference in your business. There are an endless number of things that you could be doing, but instead of getting bogged down, figure out which one or two things to focus on that will get you to your goal the fastest, and avoid or delegate all the rest. Remember, prioritizing the top 20% will make 80% of the difference.

The problem with most goals is they imply happiness only at the end of the goal.

But if you tweak the way you word it to yourself, then every time you take an action toward that goal you have accomplished it. Action, therefore, is the goal.

Chapter 17

Stand in the Gap

And I sought for a man among them, that should make up the hedge, and stand in the gap before me for the land, that I should not destroy it: but I found none.

—Ezekiel 22:30

In America today, there is a sense of foreboding and fear for the future of our country in the hearts of many people. We talk about the leaders and politicians of our country and bemoan and lament many of the decisions they make, with the average American being cynical of the politicians and leaders of our nation.

So as a Christian, what is the responsibility that I should assume to make a difference, to make the change we want to see?

How should I act? The real test of the strength of a nation does not lie with the decisions of the leaders or the politicians of the nation. It lies with the Christians of the nation.

I believe the reason America is so strong is because there are many leaders in business and government who are Christians. And there are thousands of Christians who pray for our nation every day. And that has an incredibly profound effect on our nation!

In Ezekiel 22:30 it says, "And I sought for a man among them, that should make up the hedge, and stand in the gap before me for the land, that I should not destroy it ..." It is easy to look at our politicians and leaders and blame them for the problems we face in America. I believe we need to look at our own hearts and make sure our relationship with Jesus is pure. Then he will hear us and listen to our prayers. In James 5:16 it says, "... The effectual fervent prayer of a righteous man availeth much."

We need to stand in the gap for those who are hurting. We need to stand in the gap for orphans. We need to stand in the gap for those who have lost a loved one. We need to stand in the gap for the oppressed. We need to stand in the gap and help the lost find Jesus, and we need to stand in the gap and pray earnestly for our nation!

Chapter 18

Walk in Your Purpose

But ye are a chosen generation, a royal priesthood, an holy nation, a peculiar people; that ye should shew forth the praises of him who hath called you out of darkness into his marvelous light.

—1 Peter 2:9

What is the price you will pay for the future you desire? Because there is always a price. I believe value must always be a guiding factor in what we are willing to pay.

Many people will pay the price of letting go of their values to get what they want. For example, Judas. He got the money. But he sacrificed what was worth infinitely more than money. He sacrificed his soul and values just to get more money. Then he hung himself because he was so miserable with himself. He realized too late the price he paid for the money he coveted after.

This is truly a case where he loved money. "The love of money" was his destruction (1 Timothy 6:10). He coveted money, and it destroyed him.

In Mark 8:36, it says, "For what shall it profit a man, if he shall gain the whole world, and lose his own soul?" You see, Judas lost his soul. Luke 9:25 says, "… and lose himself, or be cast away."

Judas lost himself to greed. He threw away his values, and it destroyed him. He couldn't stand himself for what he had become in pursuit of the success he craved.

We must carefully consider the cost we will have to pay for the future we desire. Jesus is a perfect example. He understood his purpose. He knew what he was going to win in the end. But he did not try to take a shortcut to what he was accomplishing.

Now the devil comes to Jesus in Luke 4:7 and offers a shortcut to his goal, "If thou therefore wilt worship me, all shall be thine." But Jesus knew better than sacrificing his values and was willing to pay the cost of doing it right.

As it says in Luke 4:8, "... Get thee behind me Satan: for it is written, Thou shalt worship the Lord thy God, and him only shalt thou serve." He did not compromise on values just to try and achieve the goal sooner. He understood when you give up your values then you have nothing worthwhile left.

Jesus knew his purpose in life. He did not leave his song unsung or his purpose unfulfilled. He died on the cross and saved humans from sin.

When I say you don't want to leave your song unsung, I simply mean leaving the purpose that you were put on this earth for unfulfilled. One of the greatest dangers we face today is the danger of not fulfilling our purpose on this earth because of little distractions.

Most of the time people have excuses like, "I'm not qualified" or "I don't think I can do that." Or a million other worthless excuses. Let your heart burn with the desire to accomplish what God has planned for you. Be bold, be courageous, because, "… God hath not given the spirit of fear; but of power, and of love, and of a sound mind (2 Timothy 1:7).

We were given a mission when we were created as a species in Genesis 1:28 which still applies today. "Be fruitful." We need to bear much fruit!

Is your life fruitful?

Are your relationships with your wife and family fruitful?

Are your relationships with your friends fruitful?

What about your business?

Or your colleagues and clients?

Or the church?

And most of all, how is your relationship with Jesus?

Being fruitful is about bearing fruit in all areas of life. It is a way of life. As it says in Genesis 1:1, "be fruitful … and multiply."

Multiply what?

I believe we need to multiply love and compassion, empathy and grace, as well as the gifts we have been given.

Are you gifted with speech? Multiply it.

Are you able to inspire? Multiply it.

Are you good at writing? Multiply it.

Are you gifted with money? Multiply it.

And the verse goes on, "… and replenish the earth." Have children and pass on your values and gifts.

"... and subdue it and have dominion over the fish of the sea and over the fowl of the air and over every living thing that moveth upon the earth." We are called to take dominion over our surroundings and use them for fruitful living and to live our lives within the purpose we have been given.

God is glorified as we accomplish the purpose he has set for us. The Bible says in Matthew 5:14, "Ye are the light of the world ... " My question is, am I walking in that purpose? Are you?

In the end, I believe there will be many more people on Judgment Day that will be guiltier of the sin of omission than there will ever be of commission. In fact, it says in James 4:17, "Therefore to him that knoweth to do good, and doeth it not, to him it is sin."

So let's live our life with purpose, with a will, and with everything we have. Not just so our name will be remembered on earth or to become famous, but simply because what we do matters!

Don't leave your song unsung!

Acknowledgments

Every one of these people has directly or indirectly contributed to this book ...

I have to start by thanking my amazing wife. Eva, you are an absolutely amazing woman. And I really appreciate all the encouragement you have given me while supporting me in my dream of writing, while also giving valuable input on it throughout the entire process.

To Clara Lee, my incredible mom, thank you for raising me. Thank you for being the person I can always call for advice, for believing in me, and teaching me in so many ways, by showing and not just saying.

For Daniel Lee, my amazing Dad, thank you for being such a fantastic leader, raising me, and teaching me so much about the Bible and life in casual conversation. Thank you for your example and for your faith in me.

Also, a huge thank you to my sister Emma, to my brother Ervin, my brother Lester, and my brother-in-law Phillip: Thank you for reading my manuscript and pointing out errors and giving me suggestions.

I'm also very grateful to Simon Lee for hiring me when I first moved to Pennsylvania. Thank you for your leadership and friendship ever since. I have learned so much from you.

And to Charles Herbster, thank you for your incredible leadership and advice that you give at trainings and events.

I have learned so much from that. It is an honor to be working with Conklin, and being able to participate in your vision for the future of the company, and to put God back in the boardrooms of America.

A huge thank you to Steve Bonar for your leadership. I've learned so much about effective communication and leadership from you, both by observation and by training.

Rod Livesay, thank you for your leadership. Your ability to inspire with a few words without mincing the truth is truly legendary, and something I aspire to be able to do.

A huge thank you to Raymond and Nora Troyer, Jesse and Elaine Yutzy, Ervin and Ruth Lee, and all the other amazing leaders on the team. You inspire me and challenge me.

Also to Owen Shrock, thank you for encouraging me to start a podcast and for helping me get it all set up. And also your continued advice and work on the podcast. That advice has helped me develop a lot of ideas that are in the book.

Also a huge thank you to the authors and content creators who have the most influence on my leadership: John Maxwell, Myron Golden, and Jim Rohn.

Last, but definitely not least, a huge thank you to Lori Lynn, my editor and publishing coach. Your suggestions and inputs are crucial. And your wealth of experience shows in the advice you give.

About the Author

Jacob Lee is a husband and father, a business owner and podcast host, and a first-time author. His passion is to help entrepreneurs — especially young entrepreneurs — succeed in business.

He owns a commercial roofing company called I Like Roofing (ilikeroofing.com) where he serves clients over most of south Florida. A National Director with the Conklin company, he works with contractors all over the country to develop successful commercial roofing companies.

On his podcast, *Let's Get to Business with Jacob Lee*, he talks about biblical business ideas that will help individuals grow and improve themselves and their businesses.

He believes the US is a strong nation, mostly because of the entrepreneurial spirit of so many Americans. And he wants to do what he can to help individuals and the country at the same time.

Jacob and his lovely wife Eva live in Florida with their four beautiful children.

If you would like to contact Jacob, you can reach out to him through his website:

jacobdlee.com

But the honor of kings is to search out a matter.

Dedication

First and foremost, to Jesus, the author and finisher of our faith. For without him, there is no hope. And in him is all joy and wisdom.

To my wife, Eva Lee, an incredible wife and mother who has supported my love of writing and keeps encouraging me in so many ways.

To my mother, Clara Lee, who is such an amazing listener and who gave me a curiosity about life and trying new things.

To my father, Daniel Lee, who loves to talk about his faith and who stoked my love of scripture, unveiling the amazing wisdom it holds.

Section IV

Stand in the Gap & Walk in Your Purpose

www.ingramcontent.com/pod-product-compliance
Lightning Source LLC
Chambersburg PA
CBHW060333130626
46553CB00003B/997